Deadly Animals Of The World:
Poisonous and Dangerous Animals
Big & Small

SPEEDY
PUBLISHING

Speedy Publishing LLC
40 E. Main St. #1156
Newark, DE 19711
www.speedypublishing.com

Copyright 2015

Most dangerous animals
around the world look
innocent or are small in size.

The box jellyfish is an extremely toxic and dangerous species of jellyfish. Their venom is considered to be among the most deadly in the world, containing toxins that attack the heart, nervous system, and skin cells.

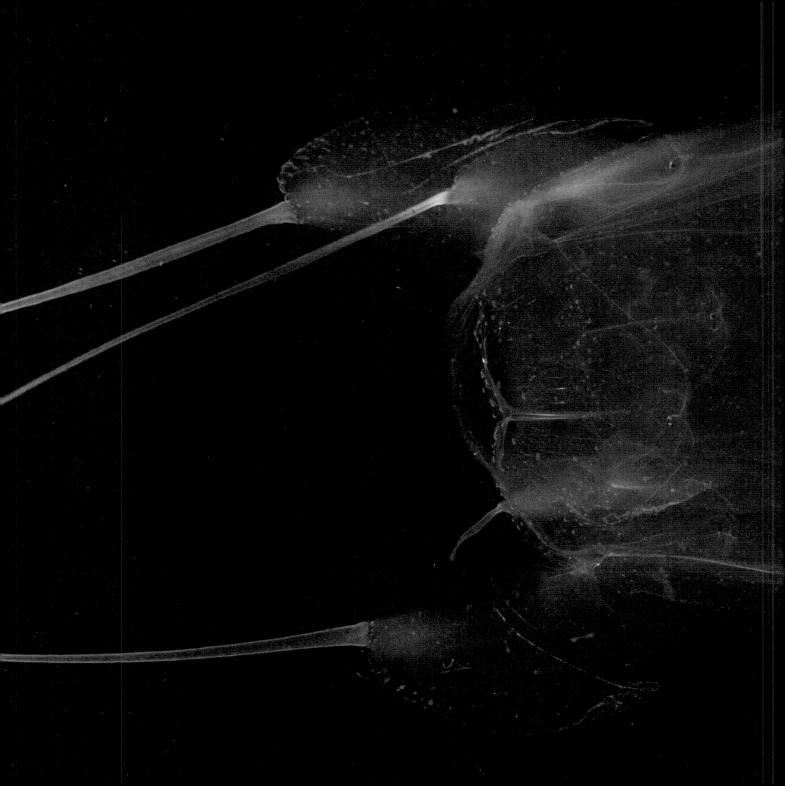

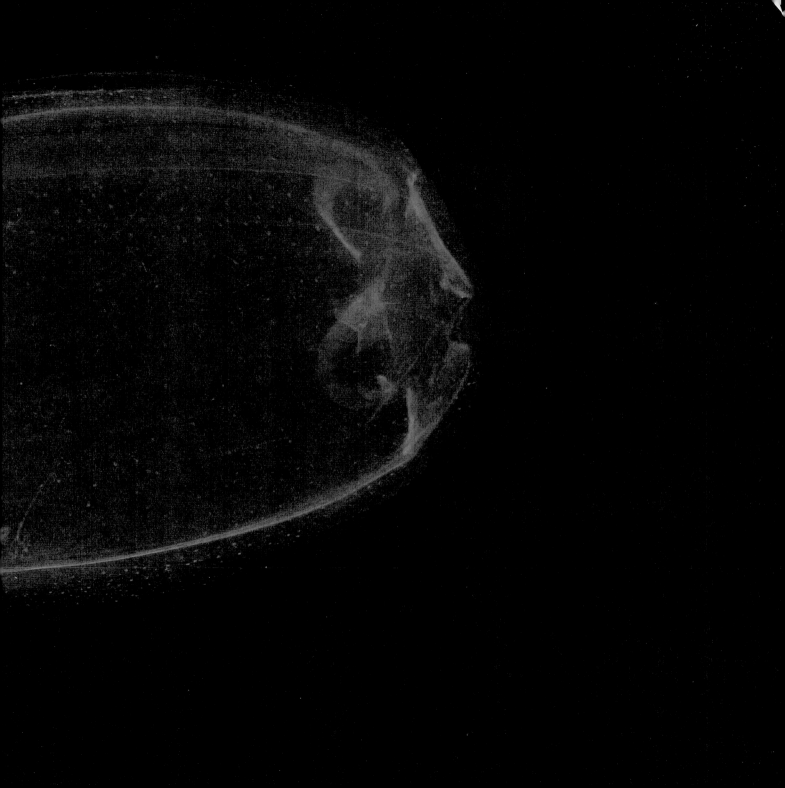

Cape buffalo have been known to charge victims without provocation. It is widely regarded as a very dangerous animal, as it gores and kills over 200 people every year.

Death Stalker Scorpion is a very dangerous species of scorpion. Its venom is a powerful mixture of neurotoxins. This venom can also cause coma, fever, paralysis, convulsions and even death.

Stonefish is the most venomous fish in the world. Venom produced by stonefish induces severe pain, paralysis and tissue necrosis. The venom of a stonefish is made of a mixture of proteins.

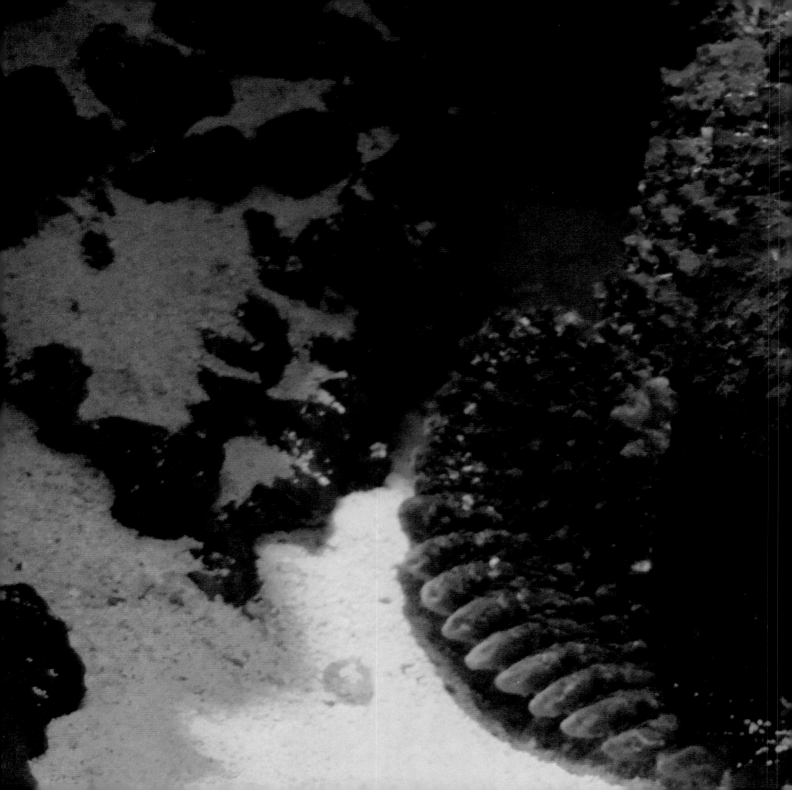

The Great White Shark is known as the most dangerous in the ocean. The great white shark has been involved in some of the most chilling attacks on humans.

The poison dart frog is considered one of the most toxic, or poisonous, species. It is believed that the frogs get their poison from an insect that they eat.

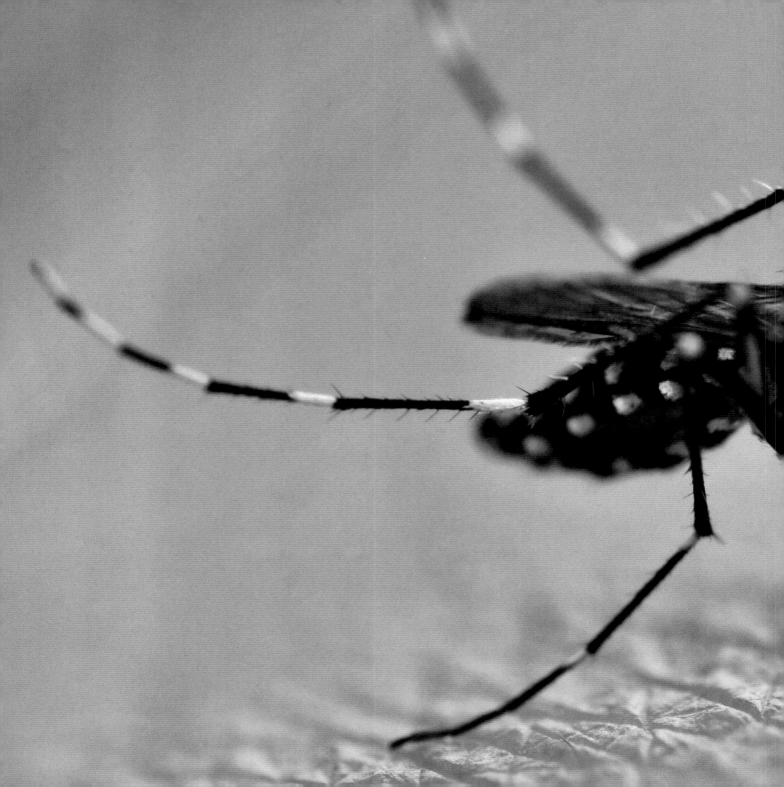

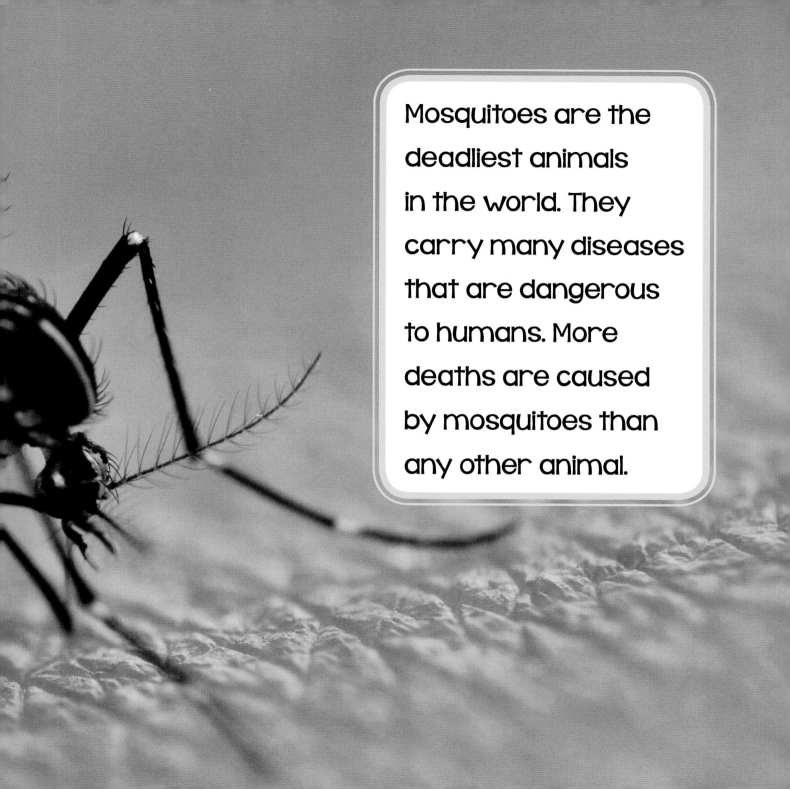

Mosquitoes are the deadliest animals in the world. They carry many diseases that are dangerous to humans. More deaths are caused by mosquitoes than any other animal.

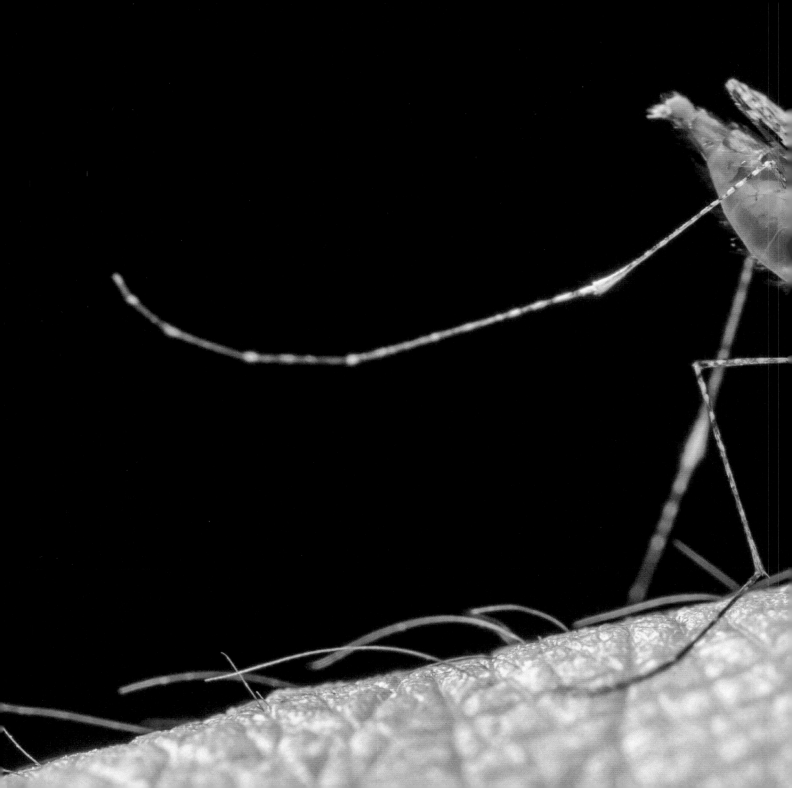

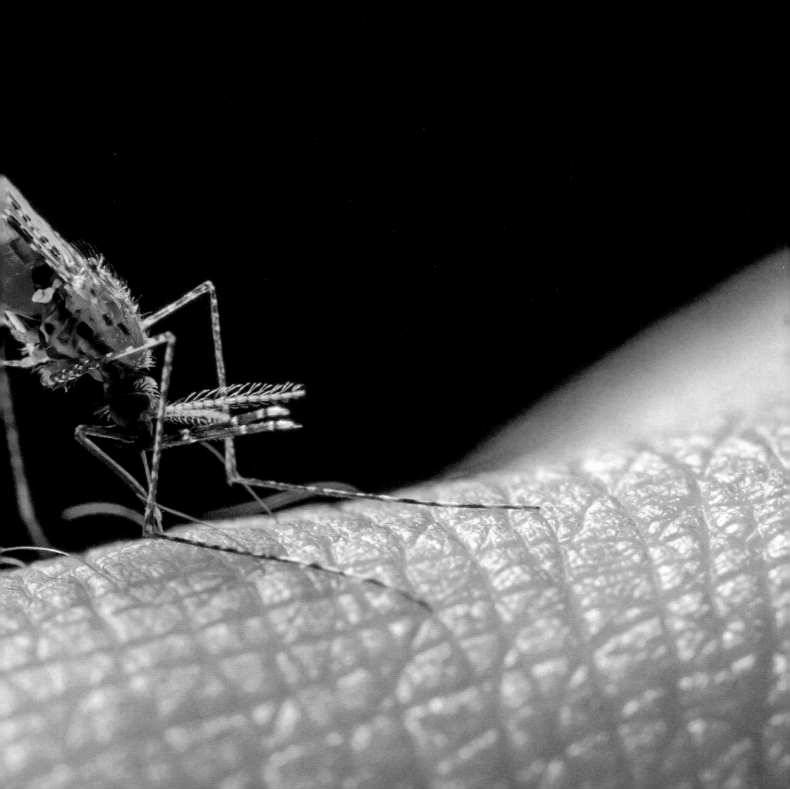